A Compendium
of Myths, Mistakes,
& Misconceptions

The
WHOLETRUTH

Gerard Del Re

Random House Reference
New York · Toronto · London · Sydney · Auckland

This book is available for special discounts for bulk purchases for sales promotions or premiums. Special editions, including personalized covers, excerpts of existing books, and corporate imprints, can be created in large quantities for special needs. For more information, write to Special Markets/ Premium Sales, 1745 Broadway, MD 6-2, New York, NY, 10019 or e-mail specialmarkets@randomhouse.com.

Please address inquiries about electronic licensing of reference products, for use on a network or in software or on CD-ROM, to the Subsidiary Rights Department, Random House Reference, fax 212–572–6003.

Visit the Random House Reference Web site: www.randomwords.com

Typeset and printed in the United States of America.
0 9 8 7 6 5 4 3 2 1

Library of Congress Cataloging-in-Publication data is available.

1st Edition
0-375-72066-9

For Patricia Del Re
always
and
Tom and Thomasina Daugherty

A Compendium
of Myths, Mistakes,
& Misconceptions

The WHOLETRUTH

by Gerard Del Re

Introduction

The Whole Truth attempts to set straight common myths, mistakes, assumptions, and misconceptions in this age of abundant (mis)information and hype. Over time, falsehoods become common knowledge and the real truth is lost.

Test yourself. Did you know that the so-called "black boxes" on airlines aren't really black? Do you think croissants and french fries originated in France? Do you think you keep the same skeleton for all of your life? Do you believe Christ was born on Christmas day? Were you told that humans evolved from apes? Are you one of the millions who think copper bracelets cure arthritis? Did you ever question that bagpipes were invented in Scotland?

Read on and find the whole truth behind the half-truths, outright lies, and silly misunderstandings. And remember to correct your friends when they're wrong. You'll do the world a favor.

Gerard Del Re

Table of Contents

Animals

Bald eagles are so named because their heads are without feathers and are bare.

Bald eagles are so named not because their heads are bare, but because the feathers on their heads are white and this color makes the eagles look bald. In addition, the word bald is derived from *balde*, which means "white" in Old English.

Bees and flies buzz because nature equipped them with a buzzing apparatus.

Bee and flies were not provided with any special apparatus that causes the insects to make a buzzing sound. The buzzing sound sometimes made by bees and flies is produced by the rapid motion of their wings moving up and down. Hummingbirds, moths, and butterflies beat their wings at a slower rate.

Elephants have a dreadful fear of mice.

Elephants' fear of mice crawling up their trunks is an old wives' tale. Many zoos attract mice that steal food from elephants, who usually ignore them. In fact, elephants are not even bothered if mice scamper over their backs as they sleep.

Live lobsters are red.

Lobsters are dark grey or blue or greenish in color when they are alive. They turn red only when they are boiled in water. Live rock lobsters are red.

Whales spout water, hence, "Thar she blows."

Whales do not blow or spout water. Upon rising from the depths of the ocean, whales exhale air through the nose openings in their heads. The great profusion of air, which appears to be water but is really vapor, is made when this warm air comes in contact with cold air.

Opossums hang in trees by their tails.

Opossums (pronounced "possums") have opposable thumbs on their hind paws and strong prehensile tails, which make them skillful tree climbers. They use their tails primarily as a fifth limb for climbing trees and carrying nest-building materials, but they cannot hang from them.

Bulls automatically attack when they see a red cape.

Contrary to popular belief, bulls do not automatically attack at the sight of a red cape. Bulls are unable to distinguish one color from another because they are color blind. They are simply attracted to anything waved in front of them and that is why they attack.

Gorillas are dangerous and violent animals.

Gorillas are not the dangerous, violent animals depicted in films such as *King Kong*. In their native habitat, gorillas are less feared than chimpanzees and other such playful animals. Gorillas are usually shy and retiring, and they are not known to initiate an attack against humans. They have also been known to mother humans who move gently upon them, embracing a person as if he or she were one of their young.

Cats should drink milk.

Cats may like milk, but milk products may cause digestive problems in many cats. In fact, many cats are lactose-intolerant, which means that they don't have the enzyme that digests lactose, a milk-sugar component of milk. A house cat may have diarrhea after drinking milk, and this drains nutrients from the animal. To that end, milk is not essential to a cat's health — in fact, it may be hazardous.

Milk snakes are so named because of their ability to suck milk directly from the udders of cows.

Milk snakes can not suck milk from the udders of cows. These snakes are so named because they are attracted to cow barns, where there is plenty of food in the form of small rats and mice.

Bloodhounds are so named because of their ability to pick up the scent of human blood.

Bloodhounds have no better gift for sniffing the scent of human blood than other breeds of dog. They are called "blood" hounds not because they are good blood sniffers, but because they were the first breed of dog to have their blood, or breeding, records maintained.

Tree worms are the pests that get into apples by boring into them.

Worms do not usually bore their way into apples. They are *born* in apples. A fruit fly punctures a growing apple, plants its eggs in the hole, and the eggs hatch, releasing tiny white worms that grow by feeding on the apple tissue. When the apple falls to the ground, the worms crawl out of the apple and develop into fruit flies that proceed to puncture apples, beginning the whole process over again.

Among the wisest creatures in the animal kingdom is the owl.

Owls are no wiser than other birds. The notion of wisdom and owls can be traced to the fact that the large eyes of this nocturnal creature were once thought to be a sign that it is omniscient. Also, owls live longer than many other kinds of birds because nature has blessed them with few natural predators. But ornithologists do not consider the owl clever, no matter how large its eyes are or how long it may live.

One can fish for red herring.

One cannot fish for red herring, since herring is not red when it's alive. It becomes reddish after being salted and smoked. The term is based on the practice of using dead fish to "throw off the scent" that hunting dogs might follow.

The prairie dog is in the canine family.

The prairie dog is not related to canines, but to squirrels and other rodents. The spunky prairie dog gets its name because it barks like a dog.

Koala bears are related to bears.

A koala is not a bear but a marsupial, a mammal with a pouch instead of a placenta. Other animals in the order Marsupialia include opossums, wombats, kangaroos, and bandicoots.

Chameleons change color to match their background.

Chameleons are lizards known for their ability to change colors. But they don't change their color to match their background. They change color as a result of changes in temperature, light conditions, or mood. They tend to turn lighter in color in cold conditions, and darker especially when they're angry. The baseline color for a chameleon is brown or green, but they can turn to an off-white, yellow, or light green.

Ladybugs
(ladybirds to the English)
are female insects.

Ladybugs are not strictly female, for gender has nothing to do with the origin of the name of this insect, a small, round bug with a spotted and bright red back. The insect gets its name from farmers who noticed its presence every year around the Roman Catholic feast of the Annunciation (March 25) and believed it was sent by the Virgin Mary, who is honored on that day.

Hummingbirds are so named because they hum.

Hummingbirds do not hum. When the tiniest of birds hovers over a flower, what one hears is the beating of their wings. Note: Hummingbirds must eat every 15 minutes to make up for the energy they expend beating their wings or they will die.

Once human hands touch a baby bird, its mother will reject it.

If a bird is placed back in its nest, the mother will be better able to care for it. The smell of human hands will not deter her.

Mosquitoes bite.

Contrary to popular belief, mosquitoes do not *bite*. Mosquitoes *stab* their victims. Born with jaws, a mosquito penetrates the flesh of its victim with its long proboscis, which is used for sucking blood as well. Note: The itch is from the mosquito's saliva. The saliva contains proteins that serve as an anticoagulant and help the mosquito to feed. The human immune system responds to the foreign proteins, and the reaction is an itch.

Fish cannot drown.

Fish can drown from any number of causes. For example, fish may drown when they swim into heavy polluted waters, mostly lakes, rivers, and streams where waste from factories robs the water of its oxygen. Fish take oxygen from the water through their gills, and the oxygen passes into the blood of the fish before circulating to its tissue. If the water is low in oxygen, the fish can't breathe and dies. Fish also drown when water is heavy with microscopic particles that get caught in a fish's gills as it swims, preventing it from breathing normally. And last, fish have drowned because of oil pollution and when objects have gotten caught in their mouths.

Cobras respond to the sound of the music of their snake charmers.

Cobras are both deaf and farsighted. The cobra responds not to the music played by the snake charmer with his flute, but to the charmer's movements. The cobra picks up the vibrations of the snake charmer with their heads and follows the motion of the flute (which it has learned serves no purpose to bite). The music of the flute is for the tourists.

The Pinto is a breed of horse.

Outside of America, the Pinto not considered a breed of horse, but a specific color of horse. It is believed that the Pinto is a descendant of Spanish horses that were brought to America in the sixteenth century. Those horses were barb (North African) stock crossed with European stock. Pinto is derived from the Spanish word *pintada*, meaning "painted," and the horses are often spotted with brown and white patches. Pintos became officially established as a breed in America in 1963, to some controversy in horse breeding circles.

When the Latin A.D. (*anno Domini*, meaning "In the year of the Lord") is seen in the lowercase — a.d. — it means "Before the day."

When A.D. is seen in the lowercase — a.d. — it means *Ante Diem*, "before the day."

The forbidden fruit that Adam and Eve ate in the Garden of Eden was an apple.

The apple is not mentioned in Genesis, first book of the Old Testament. In fact, apples were not grown in biblical times. What is said is that Adam and Eve simply ate of the "forbidden fruit of the tree of knowledge, of good and evil" (Genesis 3:6).

Christ was born on Christmas Day (December 25).

Jesus Christ was probably not born on December 25, the date on which the Christian world commemorates his birth. The actual date of Christ's birth is not known. Theories abound as to the time of year that Jesus was born. Many scholars believe the date had to be the spring or fall, when shepherds would have had their sheep and lambs out at night under the stars. The Catholic Church gradually began to set Christian feast days shortly after 313, when Constantine the Great declared Christianity an official religion. Easter was placed on the Christian calendar in A.D. 325. In the year A.D. 350, Pope Julius I set the official date of Christ's birth at December 25. Julius I picked December 25 because he wished Christ's birth to replace the pagan feast of Mithra that was celebrated on that day.

The Trojan Horse was built by the Trojans.

The Trojan Horse was built by the Greeks, not the Trojans. During the legendary ten-year Trojan War, the Greeks left the horse at the gates of the City of Troy. The horse was giant, wooden, and contained a secret compartment in which Greek soldiers hid. According to the story, the Trojan people were jubilant over the gift and rolled the horse into their city. They looked upon the gift as a Greek concession (thanks to Sinon, a Greek spy) and celebrated for many days. When at last the Trojans slept, the Greeks exited from the secret compartment and one by one killed the Trojan guards. Within days, Troy was conquered. The expression "Beware Greeks bearing gifts" also comes from this event.

The great line of Roman Emperors began with Julius Caesar.

Julius Caesar did not take the title emperor, but dictator, a title he chose in 44 B.C., almost a year after having been elected to this fifth consulship. It was Caesar Augustus who in 29 B.C., after the assassination of Julius Caesar in 44 B.C., took the title of imperator, from which the word *emperor* is derived. Among Augustus's far-reaching reforms was to return Rome from a military dictatorship (as presided over by his predecessor Julius Caesar) to constitutional rule.

When people were crucified in Roman times, the nails were hammered through the hands, as seen on replications of Christ on a crucifix and works of art.

The nails, as presented by Roman laws governing executions in Imperial Rome, were hammered through the wrists of the crucified, not the hands. This was done to prevent the victim from falling from the cross. Early in the Republic period of Rome, at the time of Spartacus, the procedure for cross executions was to tie the arms to the crossbeams, but the criminal took too long to expire. The famous Old Testament lines as spoken by King David have created the mistaken notion : "They have pierced my hands and my feet, they have numbered all my bones."

The Colosseum, the great Roman amphitheater, was the original name of the outdoor theater when it was completed in A.D. 80.

The Colosseum, as the great Roman amphitheater is commonly known today, was not known by that name until the Middle Ages. The actual name of the theater was the Flavian Amphitheater, named after the emperors of the Flavian dynasty that funded it (Vespasian, Titus, and Domitian). The Flavian Amphitheater acquired its more popular name after the *colossal* statue of the emperor Nero that stood near the theater.

The catacombs were specifically used by the early Christians to escape Roman persecutions.

Catacombs, complex underground tunnels and rooms, were specifically used for burials. They were found in many parts of the Roman Empire, and the notion that Christians used such places to escape persecution may have been cultivated by the fact that early Christians martyrs were buried in the catacombs. Bodies were placed in niches within the walls. There were Jewish catacombs as well, built for the same purpose. Literature such as *Quo Vadis* and movies have popularized this myth.

Lady Godiva rode naked on a horse through the streets of Coventry.

Lady Godiva was indeed a real person who lived in the eleventh century. She was the wife of Leofric, earl of Mercia, a powerful and wealthy nobleman. She and her husband were patrons of the arts and she took a special interest in Greek and Roman art. According to legend, she urged her husband to tax the peasants less so they would have more money to develop an interest in the higher arts. He dared her to ride naked, and in exchange, he would cut taxes. After all, Roman and Greek art celebrated the naked human body. She agreed. A nice story, but the earliest written record of it comes more than a century after Godiva's death from Roger of Wendover, a scribe known for exaggeration and politically biased embellishment. Over the centuries, the tale has grown more colorful and increased tourism to Coventry, which has unsurprisingly embraced the legend.

The Bubonic Plague originated in Europe.

Although the Bubonic Plague spread across Europe and wiped out one-fourth of the continet's population, it did not originate in Europe. The disease, which was caused by bacteria carried by fleas and rats, appeared in China as early as 1334 and quickly traveled to India, Syria, and Mesopotamia via trade routes. Its earliest known introduction to Europe occurred in 1347 in the form of germ warfare when a Kipchak army (a Mongolian tribe) besieged a trading post in Genoa and catapulted corpses of its own diseased men over the walls of the fortified city. From there the plague spread throughout the rest of Europe, ultimately infecting 25 million Europeans.

Christopher Columbus set out to prove that the Earth is round, not flat.

Educated people in Columbus's time knew that the Earth was round (medieval maps were *not* labeled "here there be dragons"). The controversy was over the size of the Earth. Incidentally, Columbus underestimated the size of the Earth by one fourth and thought that he would reach Asia. Instead, he reached the Americas.

Christopher Columbus discovered America in 1492.

Christopher Columbus did not discover America. First of all, the Native Americans were already there. Moreover, Columbus was not the first European to set foot on American soil. The Vikings, led by Leif Ericson, were the first Europeans to land on the coast of North America around A.D. 1000. Christopher Columbus landed on the island of San Salvador (or Samana Cay, among other possibilities) in 1492, thinking he had reached the East Indies.

The Puritans came to America because they were persecuted in England.

The Puritans were not pilgrims, and they did not suffer religious persecution in England. Unlike the Pilgrims, the Puritans did not seek to separate from the Church of England. Instead, they sought a greater reformation of the Church of England, with the intention of "purifying" it from elaborate forms and ceremonies.

The Pilgrims celebrated Thanksgiving every year with the Indians on the fourth Thursday of November.

Thanksgiving, an annual event occurring on the third Thursday of November, was never celebrated by the Pilgrims. To them, a thanksgiving was a religious event for which they would go to church and praise God. The celebration that first took place in 1621 between the pilgrims and Wampanoag did not happen every year and was never called a thanksgiving by the pilgrims, because it was a secular event, not a religious one. Thanksgiving was adopted as an official secular holiday by Abraham Lincoln in 1863.

The Salem women accused of being witches in 1692 during the Salem Witch Trials were burned at the stake.

The popular belief that the unfortunate women accused of being witches in Salem, Massachusetts, were executed by being burned at the stake is not true. The accusations of English-American clergyman Samuel Parris set the stage for the Salem Witch Trials in the Massachusetts Colony, and after two years nineteen men and women were hanged, and one man was pressed to death — but none were burned at the stake. Many of the women were sent to their death on the testimony of Ann Putnam, aged twelve, who later recanted. The notion that the women were burned at the stake may be traced to St. Joan of Arc who, after being accused of being a witch, was burned at the stake in 1431.

During his midnight ride through the Boston countryside (April 18, 1775), Paul Revere shouted, "the British are coming."

Paul Revere did not alert the early American militia, called Minutemen, with the cry, "the British are coming." In fact, many colonists still considered themselves to be British. Instead, Paul Revere set out on his horse, shouting, "the regulars are out" (the "regulars" were British infantry soldiers). He rode from Boston to Lexington, Massachusetts.

Betsy Ross designed the first American flag.

Indeed, Betsy Ross, born Elizabeth Griscom (1752–1836), was a seamstress who had made flags during the American Revolution. But there is no proof that she designed the first American flag known as the Stars and Stripes. Official records have not confirmed Ross as the designer of the first American flag, despite what old schoolbooks claim. It will probably never be known who designed the first American flag, which was first raised on January 2, 1776. The 13 stripes on the American flag represent the original 13 colonies — which later became states.

HISTORY

All the signers of the Declaration of Independence penned their signatures on the historical document on July 4, 1776.

Only one of the founding fathers of the United States signed the Declaration of Independence on July 4, 1776. The signer, John Hancock, president of the Congress, and only Mr. Hancock, affixed his name to the document on July 4, 1776, for legal reasons. The other signatures were added later.

The guillotine — infamous as a means of punishment during the French Revolution (1789–1793) — was invented by Dr. Joseph Guillotin.

Dr. Joseph Guillotin did not invent the instrument of capital punishment that bears his name. The decapitation device infamous during the French Revolution had been in use since the Middle Ages, and Guillotin simply wrote an article advocating its use as a humane form of capital punishment. When the machine was first demonstrated to King Louis XIV, the king suggested the blade be adjusted to an oblique angle. Louis XIV and his queen, Marie Antoinette, were later to lose their own lives to the machine. As for Dr. Guillotin, he died in his sleep. Incidentally, the guillotine kept its name despite an attempt by the Guillotin children to change it. In the end, the family decided to change their name.

The Battle of Waterloo was fought at Waterloo, Belgium.

The battle that came to be known to the world as the Battle of Waterloo, and which marked the end of the French emperor Napoléon, never happened at Waterloo. The famous battle took place on June 18, 1815, and should rightly be called the Battle of La Belle-Alliance, because La Belle-Alliance, Belgium, was the actual scene of the battle. The battle received its name because of General Wellington's own tradition of naming his battle after the place where he had spent the previous night, which in this case was Waterloo, some seven miles north of La Belle-Alliance.

The Battle of the Alamo, fought for Texas independence, solely concerned the territory that is present-day Texas.

The territory that today makes up the state of Texas was not the only piece of land over which the Battle of the Alamo was fought. In 1836, when the Alamo conflict occurred, the territory of contention (the Republic of Texas) was what is present-day Texas as well as parts of New Mexico, Oklahoma, Colorado, Kansas, and Wyoming.

U.S. currency has always included the phrase, "In God we trust."

"In God we trust" appeared only on the 2-cent piece after the coin was introduced in 1864. An act of Congress in May 1908 required the phrase to be placed on all coins. President Theodore Roosevelt, who held the opinion that putting God's name on a coin is sacrilegious, tried to overrule the Treasury Bill law, but in 1908 Congress overruled him. The phrase "In God we trust" did not appear on paper currency until 1954.

President Abraham Lincoln wrote his famous Gettysburg Address on the back of an envelope while traveling on a train to Gettysburg.

Lincoln's famous Gettysburg Address—a speech delivered during the American Civil War as a dedication to those killed in the Battle of Gettysburg—was written on White House stationery, not the back of an envelope. It had been drafted at least twice, and Lincoln improvised a bit during the speech. It was also not written on a train—the ride then would have been too bumpy.

Abraham Lincoln started the Civil War over the issue of slavery.

Abraham Lincoln didn't start a war over slavery; many times he made statements similar to the one he made in 1862 to Horace Greeley, "My paramount object in this struggle is to save the Union, and is not either to save or destroy slavery." Although historians still do not agree on all the causes of the Civil War, the basic issues boil down to the fact that in nineteenth-century America, the South remained almost completely agricultural, with an economy and a social order largely founded on slavery and the plantation system. The North, with its own great agricultural resources, was always more advanced commercially, and was also expanding industrially. The North, for economic and political reasons, did not want the South to secede from the union.

Mrs. O'Leary's cow started the great Chicago fire of 1871.

The great Chicago fire that took more than 250 lives and ruined 3.5 square miles in the heart of the city of Chicago was at one time attributed to a cow belonging to Mrs. Catherine O'Leary. The cow allegedly kicked over a lantern in the woman's barn. But the story isn't true — it's a fallacy invented by police reporter Michael Ahern, as he was to later admit, to make his coverage of the fire more interesting. The O'Leary barn and house suffered little fire damage. Historians also suspect that the story was a product of anti-Irish, anti-Catholic prejudice. No one knows the real cause of the fire, although it did indeed start in the vicinity of the O'Leary farm. Simultaneous fires in disparate towns in neighboring states point to dry weather conditions or even a meteor firestorm from the Biela Comet. In 1997, the Chicago City Council officially exonerated Catherine O'Leary from blame.

The Wright Brothers made aviation history on December 17, 1903, with the world's first engine-powered flight at Kitty Hawk, North Carolina.

The engine-powered flight in a heavier-than-air machine didn't take place at Kitty Hawk, but at Kill Devil Hill, about 4 miles south of Kitty Hawk. The flight lasted 12 seconds. Kitty Hawk had the only post office in the area and other Wright Brothers flights have taken place there, two reasons why many people believe the first flight took place there. Other claims of first flight include Gustave A. Whitehead near Bridgeport, Connecticut, on August 14, 1901, and Richard Pearse in New Zealand in March of 1902.

Adolph Hitler was the last führer of Nazi Germany.

Adolph Hitler was not the last führer of Nazi Germany. Hitler was succeeded in late April 1945 by Karl Dönitz. At the time, Dönitz was chief naval commander. Appointed führer by Hitler, he held on to power for 23 days, long enough to complete the Baltic sealift of more than 2 million Germans from the eastern districts of Germany before the Russian occupation. Those Germans were to live in freedom. Dönitz enjoyed a splendid military career before becoming führer. As an admiral, he spearheaded the drive to make German sea power a mighty force from 1935 to 1943. Karl Dönitz was a soldier endowed with one of the most brilliant military minds in the World War II military and was responsible for making Germany's submarine force second to none. He was given a 10-year sentence at the Nuremberg Trials. Upon his freedom from Spandau, Dönitz lived quietly in West Germany until his death of a heart attack on December 24, 1980, at age 89.

The Nazis invented the swastika.

The swastika, a symbol used during Hitler's Third Reich and still used by the party, was not designed by the Nazis. In fact, it existed long before Germany was called Germany. In ancient times, the swastika was known as a Buddhist symbol of health and healing, and it was used as a symbol by many cultures. It was well known in Persia and in Greece, and is found woven into Persian carpets and on Greek coins of ancient times. It was also used during the Christian persecutions in the first and second centuries to hide the cherished symbol of the cross.

The term *Nazis*, an abbreviation for the National Socialist German Worker's Party, was the original abbreviation of the political party established by Adolf Hitler in 1933.

The original abbreviation for Hitler's party was Nasos, not Nazi. Nazi was first used in lieu of Nasos by German author Konrad Heiden, who used it satirically because *nazi* in Bavarian means simpleminded. Somehow, Heiden's slur caught on and as Hitler's party grew it become known as the Nazi party, not the Nasos party. By 1935, *Nasos* was not used anymore, even by Hitler.

The term *D-Day* was first used during World War II, referring to the invasion at Normandy, France, on June 6, 1944.

The term *D-Day* was not first used in World War II, but during World War I. During World War I, the *D* in D-Day stood for *Day* ("Day-Day") and was used as the code for the Allied Offensive at Saint Mihiel (September 12, 1918). In World War II, none of the Allies — France, Great Britain and the U.S. — agreed on what the *D* in D-Day actually stood for.

The sinking of the *Lusitania* was a major factor in bringing the United States into World War I.

A passenger vessel of the Cunard lines, SS *Lusitania* was sunk off the coast of Ireland by a pair of torpedoes from a German submarine on May 7, 1915, with 1,198 lives lost — 128 Americans among them. The fact that so many Americans lost their lives, many woman and children among them, sparked anger across America, whipping up sentiment for a U.S. entry into World War I. However, in a formal protest to the German government, the U.S. denunciation was quite placid, almost of a pacifist nature, due in part to a pacifist Secretary of State, William Jennings Bryan. The Germans resumed sinking unarmed passenger ships in November 1916. On February 3, 1917, the United States severed diplomatic ties with Germany, which was followed a few hours later by the sinking of the USS *Housatonic* by a German submarine. On April 6, 1917, the United States declared war on Germany, almost two years after the *Lusitania* sinking.

Literature
& Theater

The world is fortunate that the great philosopher Socrates wrote down his observations, which would otherwise be lost.

Socrates never wrote down a single word of his philosophy; his teachings were recorded by his student, Plato. Plato usually wrote dialogue between Socrates and some other person, with Socrates speaking in the present tense, as if Socrates were merely speaking to an audience in the marketplace. Plato's writings on the conversations of Socrates must have sharpened his own thoughts, for Plato became a famous philosopher in his own right.

The word *Divine* in Dante Alighieri's poem *Divine Comedy* (1320) was the poet's original title for the work.

Dante titled his famous poem simply *Comedy* (*Commedia* in Italian). Later, a translator added the word *divine*.

In Shakespeare's time, women and girls played the parts of Juliet, Lady Macbeth, and other female characters in Shakespeare's plays.

In the sixteenth century, males played female parts on the British stage. Women were not allowed to perform. Young boys often played the female parts, dressed in women's clothing and dolled up with careful makeup. In Britain, women were allowed to perform on stage beginning in the seventeenth century.

In the original *Cinderella*, Cinderella's slippers are made of glass.

The oldest known rendition of Cinderella has her wearing slippers made of fur, not glass. The slip happened in an early translation from the French *pantouffles en vair* (fur slippers) for *pantouffles en verre* (glass slippers).

In the play *She Stoops to Conquer* by Oliver Goldsmith (1773), the famous quote by character Tony Lumpkin is "Ask me no questions and I'll tell you no lies."

In *She Stoops to Conquer*, the famous line is: "Ask me no questions and I'll tell you no fibs."

Noah Webster's best-seller in his lifetime was the dictionary that still bears his name.

Noah Webster's best-seller while he lived was not the dictionary, but *The Blue Backed Speller*, published in 1783. By 1800, the famous spelling book had surpassed the million mark in copies sold.

Frankenstein is the monster of Mary Shelley's famous gothic tale (1818).

Frankenstein was not the name of the monster, but rather the name of its inventor, Dr. Victor Frankenstein. The monster, famously portrayed by actor Boris Karloff, had no name and was referred to as "Frankenstein's monster." Dr. Frankenstein was able to galvanize his creation into life and in the end became one of its victims.

Grimm's fairy tales were written by Jakob and Wilhelm Grimm.

Unlike Hans Christian Anderson whose fairy tales come from his own fertile imagination, the Grimm Brothers, Jakob and Wilhelm, did not write their fairy tales, but collected them from German folk sources, compiling them into volumes titled *Grimm's Fairy Tales* (1812–1815).

The Sugar Plum Fairy is a character in E.T.A. Hoffman's famous tale *Nutcracker and the Mouse-King.*

The character Sugar Plum Fairy who appears in the Nutcracker ballet is not found in E.T.A. Hoffman's tale *Nutcracker and the Mouse-King* (1816), nor was the original ballet (1892) based on Hoffman's version. Hoffman, in spite of his genius for inventing unusual characters, never envisioned a character like the Sugar Plum Fairy. The original ballet was based on the writings of the great French author Alexandre Dumas, who wrote *The Three Musketeers*. Based on Hoffman's tale, Dumas wrote *The Nutcracker of Nuremburg* in 1845 for the children of France. But Dumas's version was also without a character known as the Sugar Plum Fairy. The marvelous character was a product of the imagination of Ivan Alerandrovic Vsevolojky, the director of the Imperial Theater in St. Petersburg. He wrote the scenario from Dumas's version, taking the liberty of adding the Sugar Plum Fairy (personified by music from a celesta, an instrument patented only two years prior) and a cavalier to make the ballet more interesting to the composer, Peter Illyich Tchaikovsky, and choreographers Marius Petipa and Lev Ivanov.

The title of Clement Clarke Moore's famous Christmas poem is "'Twas the Night Before Christmas" (1822). The last line of the poem is "Merry Christmas to All and to All a Good Night!"

The title of Clement Clarke Moore's famous Christmas poem is "A Visit from St. Nicholas." The last line is "*Happy* Christmas to All and to All a Good Night!" "'Twas the Night Before Christmas" is the first line of the Christmas classic.

Dr. Jekyll and Mr. Hyde (1886) is the correct title of Robert Louis Stevenson's novel.

Dr. Jekyll and Mr. Hyde is the title of many films based on the famous Robert Louis Stevenson tale. *Strange Case of Dr. Jekyll and Mr. Hyde* is the correct title of the Stevenson work.

Count Dracula
never existed in real life.

Bram Stoker's *Dracula* (1897) is based on the life of one of history's strangest and cruelest human beings. Stoker's novel pales beside the actual man who was possessed with vile and almost unspeakable obsessions. Having escaped from his treacherous Ottoman captors in 1448, Prince Vlad Dracula fled first to Moldavia before he settled in Transylvania in Romania. Prince Vlad Dracula was soon known for his butchery and madness. It wasn't long before Dracula became known by the name of Vlad Tepeș or Vlad the Impaler because of the numerous severed heads which he exposed on his property, heads impaled on lances. His temperament swung from fits of rage to bestial laughter. It is not true that he drank blood, but his castle dungeons were the scene of torture and mayhem. He often enticed poor women and men to his castle where hospitality was promised; these hapless souls were never to be seen alive again except as heads impaled on staffs. Count Dracula's wicked life came to an end in 1477 at age 45, in a battle outside Bucharest, Romania.

Gertrude Stein wrote, "A rose is a rose is a rose" in her famous poem "Sacred Emily."

Author Gertrude Stein did not say "A rose is a rose is a rose" in her famous poem "Sacred Emily" (1913). Instead, she wrote "Rose is a rose is a rose." The difference is critical. Stein could have been writing about a person, not a flower, in this abstract poem.

The phrase "Elementary, my dear Watson" is a famous line in Sir Arthur Conan Doyle's tales about Sherlock Holmes.

Nowhere in any of the detective tales of Sir Arthur Conan Doyle is there found the widely used phrase, "Elementary, my dear Watson." Both parts, however, do appear separately in different texts. The phrase became popularized when the books became movies, beginning in 1929 with *The Return of Sherlock Holmes*.

The "Thin Man" in Dashiell Hammett's famous mystery novel of the same name is the super detective who solves murders.

The "Thin Man" is not a detective but a murder suspect who ends up being a murder victim in *The Thin Man* (1934). Nick and Nora Charles are the detectives. The two characters in the Hammett novel were made famous by actors William Powell and Myrna Loy in six films.

Johann Sebastian Bach, famous baroque composer, was renowned for his music during his lifetime.

Johann Sebastian Bach (1685–1750) was beloved in his native Germany not for his compositions, but for his talent as a virtuoso organist and his expertise in organ mechanics. The composer of "St. Matthew Passion," "Mass in B Minor," "Goldberg Variations," "Christmas Oratorio," and other compositions was dead some one hundred years before his works were revived in the nineteenth century by Felix Mendelsohn.

Handel's *Messiah* was written to be performed at Christmas, preferably during a church service.

When George Friedrich Handel (1685–1759) wrote his famous oratorio *Messiah* (1742), it was performed strictly at Eastertime and continued to be performed at that time while the composer lived. The bulk of the massive work comprises "Eastertide," parts two and three. Part two tells of Christ's Crucifixion and Resurrection, and this part also contains the famous "Hallelujah Chorus". Part three concerns Christ's ministry and its promise to all believers. Only Part one concerns Christ's birth. *Messiah* (sometimes erroneously called *The Messiah*) was intended to be entertainment, and it was not written to be performed at church services. The composer himself was the first to conduct the work, on April 13, 1742, just before Easter, in Ireland. Handel would conduct his *Messiah* many times thereafter, and for the last time on April 6, 1759, a week before Easter. After his death (he collapsed while conducting eight days later), the work gradually slipped into the Christmas festival.

Mozart sold most of his compositions, making him a wealthy man.

In his lifetime, Mozart (1756–1791) sold only 20 of the 600 or so works he composed. From this, Mozart was hardly wealthy, and the wealth he accumulated was quickly lost because Mozart was a compulsive gambler. Dead at 35, he was buried in a wooden coffin in a plot with four or five other people; a wooden marker was used to identify the grave. Although this is the kind of burial many now associate with poverty, it was the standard practice in the eighteenth century for middle-income families in Austria.

Beethoven's "Moonlight Sonata" for piano, Opus 27, was named by the composer.

The great composer Ludwig von Beethoven did not nickname his famous Opus 27 piano sonata "Moonlight Sonata." The work composed in 1801 was heard by poet Ludwig Rellstab, who in 1832 described the music as being like moonlight shining on Lake Lucerne, and the description stuck. When Beethoven wrote Opus 27 he was deeply in love with the 17-year-old Countess Giulietta Guicciardi, and he dedicated the piece to her.

Composer Frederic Chopin, beloved for his beautiful nocturnes, created that musical form.

Frederic Chopin I (1810–1849) adopted the nocturne style of music from its inventor, John Field, an Irish pianist and composer who wrote the first nocturnes (which mean "of the night"). Due to professional jealousy, Field and Chopin were not friends.

Francis Scott Key wrote the words and music to "The Star Spangled Banner," the U.S. national anthem. The song became the national anthem immediately after it was conceived in 1814.

Francis Scott Key (1780–1843) was not a musician — he was an attorney. Key wrote only the words to what was first titled "Defence of Fort M'Henry," beginning with "O say can you see....." The music itself is that of an old British drinking song ("To Anacreon in Heaven") that had been adopted by American soldiers. As for Key's poem becoming the national anthem when he penned it following the war of 1812, this is a fallacy. It would be almost 120 years later, in 1931, that Congress passed legislation officially adopting the anthem.

The famous Unfinished Symphony of composer Franz Schubert was left unfinished because the composer died.

Composed in 1822, Franz Schubert's Unfinished Symphony was not left incomplete because of his death. Schubert went on to write another symphony after his Unfinished Symphony, leaving the latter with two instead of the standard four movements. The symphony is listed officially as Symphony No. 8 in B Minor, and it was composed when Schubert was 25 years old, six years before his death on November 19, 1828, in Vienna, Austria. Why he did not add two more movements to the work is not known. Some music historians and music scholars suggest that Schubert simply had nothing more to add to that theme.

The Christmas carol "Away in a Manger" was written by Martin Luther.

"Away in a Manger" (1886) was not written by Martin Luther (1483–1546). The credit for the creation of the lovely carol belongs to James R. Murray, a music editor who gave the credit to Martin Luther to aid in the spread of Lutheranism.

Appalachian Spring (1943), the famous musical work by Aaron Copland, was the title given to the work by the composer.

The renowned musical work today known by the poetic title of *Appalachian Spring* was given such a title not by the composer, Aaron Copland, but by dancer and choreographer Martha Graham, for whom the work was written as a result of a commission. The original title was *Ballet for Martha*. The title *Appalachian Spring*, comes from the Hart Crane poem "The Dance."

Carmen, the *Nutcracker,* and *Madam Butterfly,* were enormous successes at their premieres.

The opera *Carmen* by French composer George Bizet, which premiered on March 3, 1875, at the Opera Comique in Paris, France, was a disaster with both the critics and the audience. Audiences hooted Bizet out of the theater, while critics found the opera story (about a cigarette girl and temptress who finds tragedy at the hands of one of her lovers) repulsive. At the premiere, the singer who played Carmen lost her castanets, the tenor lost his voice, and the timpanist let go with a crashing miscue during one of the arias. The Christmas ballet *Nutcracker* did no better after its premiere at the Mariinsky Theater in Leningrad, Russia, on December 17, 1892. Russian audiences did not like the fact that children monopolized the entire first act; they also thought the Sugar Plum Fairy was too homely, even though she danced well. The composer, Peter Illyich Tchaikovsky, was devastated by the poor reception. He fired the Sugar Plum Fairy—Antoinette Dell-Era—laying most of the blame for the ballet's failure on her. The tragic opera *Madam Butterfly* by Giacomo Puccini, a love tale in a Japanese setting, was a total failure at its premiere on February 17, 1904, and nearly broke its composer's heart. Both Bizet and Tchaikovsky died without seeing their creations become beloved classics.

The musical instrument known as the concertina was invented by the French.

The concertina, a form of accordion that appears in café settings of such films as *Moulin Rouge* and *The Razor's Edge*, led many to assume the instrument is French in origin. The concertina is an instrument with a small bellows with a board at each end that holds several rows of buttons. Often confused with the accordion—which has a "keyboard" fixed on its right-hand end—the concertina was actually invented by an Englishman, Sir Charles Wheatstone. He patented his concertina in 1829. Note: The accordion, sometimes associated with the French, was also invented in another country—Germany—in 1822.

The soundtrack for the Stanley Kubrick science fiction epic *2001: A Space Odyssey* (1968) was original to the film.

The music used in the film *2001: A Space Odyssey* was composed many years before the film came out. Classical music lovers were familiar with the music, a tone poem composed by Richard Strauss in 1895–96 and entitled "Also Sprach Zarathustra," Opus 30. Kubrick was familiar with the music, but it was rarely performed prior to the film's release. Only in the context of the *2001: A Space Odyssey* film did the piece become famous.

Stereo sound (stereophonic sound) was invented for music and was first used in the 1950s when the first stereo recordings come to market.

Stereo was invented in France in 1881 and was used to improve the newly invented telephone. Stereophonic sound was introduced at the Paris Electric Exhibition by an engineer named Clement Adler. At the exhibition, visitors were able to pick up receivers and hear stereophonic sound coming from the Paris Opera some four miles away, where wires had been hooked up.

Carnegie Hall, the famous concert hall in New York City, was always known as Carnegie Hall.

Opening May 6, 1891, with Tchaikovsky as one of its guest conductors, Carnegie Hall's original name was simply Music Hall. The famous concert hall was renamed Carnegie Hall in 1898 after industrialist Andrew Carnegie, who had financed most of its construction.

Pineapples are native to Hawaii.

The pineapple is most associated with Hawaii, but it is not native to the state. The herbaceous plant that the Carib Indians called *anana*, or "excellent fruit," originally evolved in the inland areas of what is now Brazil and Paraguay and was widely transplanted and cultivated. When Christopher Columbus made his second voyage to the Caribbean in 1493, he and his crew sampled pineapples on Guadeloupe. They thought the fruit looked like a pinecone, so they dubbed it the "Pine of the Indies." Later on, the English added the word *apple* for marketing purposes. Pineapples were introduced to Hawaii (then called the Sandwich Islands) in 1790 by Captain James Cook. In 1903, James Dole started canning pineapple. Automation would later greatly improve the business. Today the pineapple industry in Hawaii is in decline as land is swallowed up by developers who are building hotels, golf courses, and the like to satisfy the state's first industry, tourism.

Oranges are indigenous to both California and Florida.

The orange is not native to Florida or California. Oranges were brought to America by the Spaniards during the Columbus expeditions. The orange is not native to Spain either, but, like all other citrus fruit, is native to Southeast Asia. Oranges were cultivated in Florida in the late sixteenth century and in California since 1769.

The potato originated in Ireland.

The potato did not originate in Ireland. The tuber was first discovered and cultivated 7,000 or more years ago by pre-Columbian farmers in the Andes mountains of South America. The Mochia, Chimu, and Inca cultures developed frost-resistant varieties called *papa*. In the early sixteenth century when the Conquistadors tramped through Peru, they brought samples of the potato back to the Old World. Around 1780, the people of Ireland adopted the rugged food crop, the first country to rely on it as a principal source of nutrition, which is why the potato is now strongly associated with Ireland. Thanks to the potato, the population of Ireland almost tripled by the nineteenth century. When the Irish potato famine hit around 1845, almost one million people died of starvation and another million left for Canada and America.

Chop suey is a dish native to China.

Chop suey is not native to China. The personal cook of Mr. Li Hong Cheng, a diplomat during President Grover Cleveland's administration, created chop suey in the United States in the 1890s. At the time, Americans mostly ate potatoes, meats, gravy, but few vegetables. Chop suey is made of small pieces of meat combined with mixed vegetables cooked in their own juices, and served over rice. The name *chop suey* means "odds and ends" in Cantonese. Chinese miners and rail workers probably invented the dish and included in it whatever ingredients were on hand. The dish became popular among all Americans and is now served everywhere, including China.

Fortune cookies originated in China.

Fortune cookies are a purely American invention, inspired by Chinese immigrants in America. The most popular story of the fortune cookie's invention is that it was by Los Angeles noodle manufacturer David Jung in the 1910s. He was inspired by ancient Chinese rebels exchanged concealed messages inside mooncakes and birth announcements in cake rolls. Jung's whimsical adaptation involved printing Confucian phrases and slipping them into sweet cookies. Other invention stories involve early twentieth-century Chinese railroad workers in California who celebrated the New Year by exchanging happy messages in cookies rather than in the traditional mooncakes. Another possible inventor is the legendary Makota Hagiwara of San Francisco, who used them by 1907 as thank-you notes. Whatever its actual origins, it is clear that the fortune cookie was created by Chinese in America, not China.

Venetian blinds were developed by Venetians.

While the name gives the impression that the shades made of slats were invented by Venetians, they were actually invented by the Japanese, who invented the shades using stalks of bamboo. The shades became very popular in the 1600s in Venice, which is why they became known as Venetian blinds.

Great Dane dogs originated in Denmark.

Great Danes, a descendent of the mastiff, boarhound, wolfhound and/or greyhound, did not originate in Denmark but in Germany in the seventeenth century. In fact, the breed's other name is Deutsche Dogge (or German Mastiff) and in 1876 it was declared the national dog of Germany. Records indicate the breed's use as a hunting dog in Germany and throughout Europe. The name comes from the story of an eighteenth-century French naturalist Comte de Buffon, who traveled to Denmark and saw a boarhound for the first time. Buffon called the dog *le Grand Danois*, or Great Dane, even though this variation originated in Germany and not Denmark. The most famous Great Dane is the character Scooby-Doo.

The croissant originated in France.

The croissant did not originate in France but in Vienna, Austria, in 1680, when Austria was at war with Turkey. According to legend, a group of Austrian bakers near the city wall were up in the wee hours of the morning, heard Turks tunneling, and sounded an alarm that subsequently led to the Turkish defeat. To celebrate the victory, the city granted a patent to the bakers to create a commemorative pastry in the shape of the crescent on the Turkish flag. *Croissant* is the French word for crescent and is an alternative name for the pastry's original Austrian name, *kipfel*. The original croissants were made from bread dough. In the early 1900s, a creative French baker made the first croissant with a dough similar to puff pastry .

French fries originated in France.

French fries are not a French dish, nor did they originate in France. In this case, "French" comes from the term "frenching," which applies to a method of preparation of foods, specifically, cutting vegetables lengthwise into strips.

Turkish baths originated in Turkey.

The Turkish bath, or *hamam*, did not originate in Turkey but in Sparta. What is referred to as a bath is really a steam room. The invention spread through Greece and Rome, then to Russia and Finland. The Finnish invented the sauna, where the humidity is more controlled.

Panama hats are named after the country where they were invented.

Panama hats were developed in Ecuador, but they got their name because Panama became a major market for the hats. The hat making industry is still centered in Ecuador where the hats are made from special palm leaves. The hat was common sun protection used by the builders of the Panama Canal. Note: Many imitations exist, and most so-called Panama hats are now not made in Ecuador but in Hong Kong.

Windmills originated in the Netherlands.

Windmills, today associated with the Netherlands, did not originate there. The windmill was conceived in Persia (now Iran) around A.D. 500–900. Its first use was apparently to pump water. Windmills emerged in China in the eleventh century (although undocumented usage may have occurred more than a millennium before this) where they were used to separate salt from the sea, grind grains, and pump water. The first windmills to appear in western Europe and Russia powered the textile industry and other manufacturing. The Dutch improved the design, including the inclusion of sails. With the introduction of steam and electric power, windmills have been forsaken by most countries, although there has been a resurgence in their popularity due to their low environmental impact. The Dutch still use windmills to drain water from the soggy land.

Tulips originated in the Netherlands.

The tulip, now an icon of the Netherlands, did not originate there but in Turkey. Its name is derived from *tulband*, the Turkish word for turban. The Turks first cultivated the tulip as early as A.D. 1, 000. Some scholars believe it was introduced to western Europe and the Netherlands by the seventeenth-century Viennese biologist Carolus Clusius. Others believe the tulip came to Europe via an Austrian ambassador to Turkey. In 1636 Holland became infamous for its "tulipmania" when the price of the flower often exceeded that of a house.

Guinea pigs are pigs from Guinea.

Guinea pigs are not related to pigs, nor are they native to Guinea in Africa. Guinea pigs are rodents and are only called Guinea pigs because of their shrill pig-like squeal. Guinea pigs were domesticated in Peru long before the Spanish conquerors arrived in South America. Like other rodents, including rats and mice, they are invaluable to research scientists. The "guinea" part of their name is attributed to the fact that Guinea was the first country to export the rodent to Europe.

The Jerusalem artichoke is from Jerusalem.

The Jerusalem artichoke is not an artichoke and it does not come from Jerusalem or any other place in the Middle East. The Jerusalem artichoke is a flower — a sunflower. Native to North America, the flower's tubers are edible and have a taste similar to artichokes. Researchers believe that Jerusalem artichokes arrived in Italy sometime before 1633 and *girasole*, the Italian word for sunflower, was later translated into the word "Jerusalem."

The Baltimore oriole is indigenous to Baltimore.

The bird known as the Baltimore oriole is not native to the city of Baltimore, Maryland. It is so named because it has the colors of the coat of arms (orange body with a black head) of the famous English statesman Lord Baltimore, founder of the state of Maryland.

The game Chinese checkers was developed by the Chinese.

The popular game known as Chinese checkers was not invented by the Chinese. The game is actually derived from an English version of the game called Halma, which was invented in the Victorian era. Introduced to America in the 1920s, it became known as Chinese checkers to make it sound more exotic.

The bagpipe is a Scottish invention.

The tuneful instrument known as the bagpipe is associated with Scots in kilts, but the Scots did not invent it. The Scots may have inherited it from the ancient Romans who used it in their cavalry, but it didn't originate in Rome either. It was developed in the Middle East as the *shawm*, a simple reed pipe blown with the mouth. As trading spread in the first century, so did the bagpipe.

Head cheese is a dairy product.

Head cheese has nothing to do with dairy products. Head cheese is jelled and seasoned meat made from pigs' feet and heads.

The principal ingredients in egg cream are eggs and cream.

Eggs and cream never met in the old-fashioned candy store egg cream, which was most popular in New York City. The egg cream was invented in 1890 by Louis Auster, a Jewish candy shop owner in Brooklyn, New York. The egg cream contains chocolate syrup, milk, and soda water. There are various theories about why the egg cream is named as it is, including the notion that Auster may have initially used eggs and cream in his drink, that it's a marketing gimmick, or that it sounds like Yiddish for "pure sweetness" or "pure cream" (*eht* means pure).

The U.S. nickel coin is so named because its principle element is nickel, and pennies continue to be made entirely of copper.

The U.S. nickel coin is mostly copper — 75 percent copper and 25 percent nickel — and is called a nickel because the coin is nickel-plated. As of 1982, U.S. pennies are no longer made mostly of copper (they were 5% zinc and 95% copper), but are now copper-coated with 97.5% zinc and 2.5% copper. The newer pennies weigh about one-fifth less than their predecessors.

The famous America's Cup yacht competition gets its name from the fact that the international yacht race originated in the United States.

The famous America's Cup yacht competition was started by the British in 1851, specifically by the Royal Yacht Squadron. The race took place around the Isle of Wight, and the schooner *America* won the 100 guinea trophy cup, hence, the name America's Cup. The notion that the America's Cup yacht race originated in the Americas results from the fact that until 1983 the United States had held on to the Cup, losing it after more than one hundred and thirty years to Australia.

The Molotov cocktail was named after Russian statesman V. Molotov and refers to the bomb thrown by Russian dissidents.

The Molotov cocktail—an easily made explosive consisting of gasoline in a bottle with a rag wick stuffed in its mouth—was named by the Finns, not the Russians. Molotov cocktails were used *against* the Russians who had invaded Finland in November of 1939, and named Molotov cocktail after the foreign minister of the U.S.S.R. at the time, Vyacheslav Molotov. Note: Finland was the only nation bordering the former Soviet Union that was not a member of the Soviet bloc.

Caesar salad is named after dictator Julius Caesar, who enjoyed sumptuous Roman banquets.

Julius Caesar, the Roman dictator, had nothing to do with the famous dish called Caesar salad. The Caesar salad is named after Caesar Cardini of Tijuana, Mexico. Mr. Cardini ran a moderately successful restaurant which he called Caesar's Place. On July 4, 1924, Prohibition-era Americans overran alcohol-rich Mexico on an American holiday. With the food caches low and a plethora of romaine lettuce, Caesar Cardini improvised a new treat with a special table preparation. It was an instant success. The salad was made from romaine lettuce, coddled eggs, croutons, and a dressing consisting of garlic olive oil, lemon juice, Worchestershire sauce, Parmesan cheese, and salt and pepper. Julia Child would confirm the dish at Caesar's Place within a couple of years. Mike Romanoff's Hollywood diner later made Caesar salad famous, with anchovies added to the mix.

Pound cake got its name because the cake was originally baked in one-pound portions.

Pound cake is not called pound cake because the cakes were once baked in pound portions—they were not. Pound cake is so named because among the common ingredients baked into each cake were a pound each of butter, sugar, eggs, and flour.

Welsh rabbit is a meat dish from Wales.

Welsh rabbit (also known as Welsh rarebit) is not a rabbit dish from Wales. It is a savory dish consisting of melted cheese with some ale on toast or crackers . According to most historians, the term Welsh rabbit was an ethnic slur, referring to the impoverished Welsh who were said to eat cheese on toast instead of rabbit meat. The term "rarebit" is now often used to avoid offending the Welsh or to clarify the common misconception that Welsh rabbit is a meat dish.

Footballs are made from pigskin.

Footballs, those used by the professionals and those used by the amateurs, are not made of pigskin. Those used by the pros in the National Football League are made from cowhide, and the pros use about 12 to 14 such cowhide balls in a each game. The footballs sold at your neighborhood sporting goods store are made from rubber or leather. Originally, the interior air bladder was a pig's bladder.

The four types of tea — green, black, white, and oolong — come from different varieties of tea plants.

Green, black, white, and oolong tea all come from the same plant, the small-leafed *Camellia sinensis* or the large-leafed *Camellia assamica*. The differences in taste and color result from the way the leaves are harvested and processed.

Caligula was the birth name of one of Rome's most infamous emperors.

The actual birth and royal name of the Roman emperor who became famous as Caligula was Caius Caesar Germanicus (12–41 B.C.). As a child, Caesar Germanicus wore child-sized versions of the solider boots *caligula* or *caligulae*—which roughly translates as "little boots." Unfortunately, Caligula grew up to be one of the most cruel and violent rulers in history. A famous motto attributed to the emperor was *oderint dum metuant* ("Let them hate so long as they fear").

There was only one Cleopatra, Cleopatra, Queen of the Nile.

The most famous queen of Egypt, Cleopatra of renowned beauty, was not the only Cleopatra. There were six Cleopatras before her, all related to one another and all belonging to the mighty Egyptian dynasty known as the Ptolemy Dynasty. Cleopatra I was the daughter of Antiochus, King of Syria — her name is found in the hieroglyphics on the Rosetta Stone. She was followed by Cleopatra II, her daughter who married her own brother, Ptolemy VI, and later then her other brother, Ptolemy VIII; Cleopatra III, daughter of Ptolemy VI; Cleopatra IV; Cleopatra V — known as Cleopatra "Selene;" and Cleopatra VI, who gave birth to the last and most famous Cleopatra, Queen of the Nile (69 B.C.–30 B.C.). The death of this last queen — under mysterious circumstances after her ill-fated love with Mark Antony — brought an end to the Cleopatras.

Cleopatra was Egyptian.

Cleopatra was Greek, not Egyptian. Although her family lived in Egypt for more than three hundred years, to the Egyptians she was Greek. Indeed, most of her family did not even speak Egyptian. Her ancestor was the general Ptolemy who served under Alexander the Great. When Alexander died, Ptolemy and two other generals divided his empire and Ptolemy gained Egypt.

St. Patrick was born in Ireland and he rid the country of its snakes.

Known as the Apostle of Ireland, St. Patrick (389?–461) was not born in Ireland, nor is there any evidence that he rid that country of its snakes. The snake legend is probably based on the fact that the snake is a Catholic symbol of Satan. The great and beloved saint of the Irish people tells us in his *Confessio*, a book written near the end of his life, that he was born in the village of Bannavem Taberniae, in what is now believed to be part of Great Britain. When young Patrick, then named Magonus Sucatus, (changed to Patrick, it is thought, upon his ordination to the priesthood) was about 16, he was kidnapped by Irish raiders and sold into slavery. He escaped his bondage, and returned to his family estate. After his ordination as Patrick, he went back to Ireland and was instrumental in converting the people to Christianity.

Good King Wenceslas was a king.

Clergyman and author John Mason Neale wrote the popular Christmas hymn "Good King Wenceslas":

Good King Wenceslas looked out on the Feast of Stephen,
When the snow lay round about, deep and crisp and even.
Brightly shone the moon that night, though the frost was cruel,
When a poor man came in sight, gathering winter fuel.

Despite Neale's carol, Wenceslas was a duke, not a king. Duke Wenceslas of Bohemia reigned in the early tenth century. The carol by Neale recounts the legend of the good king who "looked out on

the Feast of Stephen" (Dec. 26) and saw a poor man gathering wood for fire to keep himself warm; the king was touched by the man's plight and presented him with wine and logs. It was this saintly man's life that inspired Neale to write his carol. Duke Wenceslas in real life took a vow of poverty, but his generous spirit and saintly ways could not survive amid court intrigues, including a mother, Dragomira, who would not rest until she regained the throne, which was lost when her son put his title into the protective hands of the German people. Misfortune fell upon the good duke when he was slain by his brother, Boleslaw, and his gang of assassins.

Francis was the birth name of the renowned St. Francis of Assissi.

Giovanni (John) Francesco Bernardone, born in 1182 at Assissi in Umbria, Italy, was the birth name of the saint famous for his love of animals, particularly birds. His father, a wealthy merchant, altered his son's name to Francesco, for France, where business had led him at the time of the baby's birth. The name was immortalized when Giovanni of Assissi, known to all as Francis, became the founder of the Franciscan order.

**The philosopher Machiavelli was
a cruel, deceitful man; hence one with such
defects of character is properly
characterized as being "Machiavellian."**

Statesman and philosopher Niccolò Machiavelli (1469–1527)
was never known for being cruel or deceitful. The adjective
"Machiavellian" is based on Machiavelli's work *The Prince* (1515),
a book that describes what a ruler must do to stay in power. The
book was based on Machiavelli's experiences in the employ of
Cesare Borgia, who survived as a calculating tyrant. Machiavelli's
Discourses on the First 10 Books of Livy (1517) stresses the importance
of good, clean government, yet the work is hardly ever mentioned.
Machiavelli was a philosopher, not a cruel and deceitful man in
his own right.

Copernicus was the first to suggest that Earth revolves around the Sun.

Nicolaus Copernicus (1473–1543), who in 1543 introduced a heliocentric model of the Solar System, was not the first to suggest that the Sun is in the center of the system and the planets revolve around it. The Pythagorean scholar Aristarchus of Samos (310–230 B.C.) had the same idea, but those ideas were not as readily accepted at that time and his work was lost for centuries. Copernicus devised his thesis *De revolutionibus orbium coelestium* ("On the Revolutions of the Heavenly Spheres") in 1514, but publication did not occur until 1543, the year he died, and the idea was considered heretical and revolutionary even 1,800 years after Samos first conceived it. Copernicus's advantage, however, was a simple mathematical way of tracking planetary orbits that was highly accurate.

Galileo Galilei invented the telescope.

Galileo did not invent the telescope; he adapted it by increasing the instrument's magnification. There is still controversy over who actually invented it. Johannes Lippershey, a spectacle-maker from Holland, is the man whom most historians credit with the invention. In 1608 the Dutchman patented a refracting telescope and marketed it successfully.

Halley discovered the comet which bears his name.

Sir Edmund Halley (1656–1742) did not discover the comet that bears his name. Astronomers were well aware of the comet's existence before Halley was born. Halley researched reports of the comet as seen by astronomers in 1531 and 1607 and predicted that the same comet would return every 76 years. It did return in 1759 and was thus named after him.

The state of Pennsylvania is named after William Penn.

While many people, Pennsylvanians among them, believe Pennsylvania was named after William Penn, founder of the state, it was not. Pennsylvania is named after the father of William Penn, Admiral Sir William Penn (1621–70), a friend of Charles II. When King Charles II granted William Penn the charter, Penn was very flattered, but he declined the honor of having the state named after him. He was immediately informed by Charles that it was his father, and not he, that the state was named after. The "sylvania" part of the name was a reference to the forestry there.

Catherine the Great, Empress of Russia, was born in Russia and Catherine was her birth name.

Catherine the Great's original name was Sophie Augusta, not Catherine, and she was born in 1729 in Germany, not Russia. Her family were German nobles, a lineage going back to Christian I, the king of Denmark, Norway, and Sweden. In 1745 she married Peter Feodorovich, heir to the Russian throne. At that time she was christened Ekaterina Alekseevna, according to Orthodox custom. When Peter was murdered by Catherine's lover in 1762, Catherine took over the throne. Catherine learned the Russian language and became a friend and supporter of French Enlightenment thinkers such as Rousseau and Diderot. She died in 1796.

George Washington's teeth were made of wood.

George Washington (1732–99) began losing his teeth when he was quite young. He had only two left by the time he was president. He had two sets of dentures made not of wood but of hippopotamus tusk ivory inlaid with gold. In 1976, one set was stolen from a Smithsonian storage area and has never been seen again.

Napoléon was very short.

Emperor Napoléon Bonaparte (1769–1821), was not short; he was 5 feet 6 inches, which by eighteenth-century standards was about average height for a man. After Napoléon died in 1821, his body was autopsied in France, and his height was noted as 5 foot 2 inches. This measurement was in French feet (*pieds de roi*) and was not correctly converted to standard English measure until later. In English feet, Napoléon stood 5 foot 6.5 inches tall. The misconception may also have come about because Napoléon surrounded himself with tall military men.

The National Audubon Society was founded by John J. Audubon, ornithologist, who, while he lived, was fervently devoted to the conservation of wildlife, particularly birds.

The National Audubon Society was not founded by John J. Audubon (1785–1851). Today Audubon is assumed to be an environmentalist dedicated to the preservation of wildlife, particularly birds, but his life tells a different story. First, many a bird lost its life to Audubon, who was an avid hunter. Audubon's fame and good name comes from his talent as an artist. He painted pictures of birds and other animals with great depth, beauty, and realism. Lucy Audubon, John James Audobon's widow, tutored George Bird Grinnell, a founder of the early Audubon Society. Grinnell thought Audubon's name symbolized the organization's mission to protect birds and their habitats.

PEOPLE

Legends Buffalo Bill Cody, Billy the Kid, Wild Bill Hickock, Annie Oakley, and Wyatt Earp were all born in the American West.

None of the following American West legends were born in the American West. Buffalo Bill (born William Frederick Cody) was born in Le Claire, Iowa; Billy the Kid (born Henry McCarty) was born in New York City; Wild Bill Hickock (born James Butler) was born in Troy Grove, Illinois; Annie Oakley (born Phoebe Annie Oakley Moses) was born in Darke County, Ohio; Wyatt Earp (full name, Wyatt Berry Stapp Earp) was born in Monmouth, Illinois.

Helen Keller
was born
blind and deaf.

Helen Keller (1880–1968) was not born blind and deaf, but became
blind and deaf at nineteen months of age as a result of scarlet fever.

Thomas Edison invented the motion picture.

Inventor Thomas Edison (1847–1931) did not invent the motion picture. Many inventors had a hand in the development of the motion picture before Thomas Edison, beginning with the French-born inventor Louis Alme Augustin le Prince, who completed his invention of the motion picture in 1886. Prince sought and was granted a patent in 1888 for the invention of the "Successive production by means of a photographic camera of a number of images of the same object or objects in motion and reproducing the same in order of taking by means of a projector . . ." Edison simply benefited from other inventors' ideas, which go back as far as 1872 when the Englishman Eadweard Muybridge applied the principle of still photograph in motion. What Edison did was to commercially develop a film processor for which he sought to patent in 1891. The machinery was the kinetoscope (viewer) and kinetograph (shooter), which used 35 mm. film. The first public demonstration was in 1893.

Painter Vincent van Gogh cut off his entire ear.

In 1888, in Arles, France, Van Gogh (1853–90) took a razor and cut off his earlobe, not his entire ear. The earlobe excision was one act in a sequence of masochistic attacks that led to his suicide in 1890.

The late Grace Kelly was Monaco's first American princess.

Before Grace Kelly was Alice Heine, a wealthy woman from New Orleans who married Prince Albert of Monaco in 1889. Heine became Monaco's first American princess, albeit briefly, before she left Albert for a songwriter.

Charles Lindberg piloted the first nonstop transatlantic plane flight.

Charles Lindberg (1902–74) did not pilot the first nonstop transatlantic plane flight. The first nonstop transatlantic plane flight was made by Capt. John Alcock and Lt. Arthur Whitten Brown, from Newfoundland to Ireland, on June 14 and 15, 1919. Their flight took sixteen hours and twelve minutes. Charles Lindberg is famous for having made the first transatlantic *solo* flight, in the *Spirit of St. Louis*. The flight was from New York to Paris, and it took place on May 21, 1927. It earned him the nickname The Lone Eagle.

Betty Crocker, the symbol of General Mills Foods, was a real person.

Betty Crocker was not a real person. Created to be a personable symbol of General Mills Foods in 1921, portraits of what the company believes Crocker ought to look like have been modeled after real women and have been updated over the decades. The company chose the name "Betty" because it was friendly-sounding, and "Crocker" from a recently retired director (William G.) of the company.

Las Vegas oddsmaker Jimmy the Greek was born in Greece, hence his nickname

Jimmy the Greek (1923–1996), the famous Las Vegas oddsmaker, was born in Steubenville, Ohio, of Greek descent. He was born Demetrios Synodinos, but changed his name to James G. Snyder.

Adolf Hitler was a vegetarian.

At various times Hitler (1889–1945) reduced the amount of meat in his diet, primarily for medical reasons, but he never became a vegetarian. Sometimes he significantly reduced his meat consumption, but the evidence shows that he never stopped eating meat completely for any significant length of time. Stuffed squab was one of his favorite dishes.

The famous von Trapp family featured in *The Sound of Music* escaped the Nazis by trekking over the Alps, as depicted in the movie and the play.

Georg von Trapp, his pregnant wife Maria, and his seven children did not escape the Nazis by trekking across the wintry Alps as depicted in the famous musical *The Sound of Music*. Instead, in 1938, they calmly stole out of their house at night with only backpacks, boarded a train for Italy, and booked passage on a ship to the United States. Their flight was managed by a Catholic priest, Monsignor Franz Wagner, a family connection.

Babe Ruth closed out his long and spectacular baseball career with the New York Yankees.

Babe Ruth (1895–1948) closed out his career in 1935 with the old Boston Braves in the National League, having been traded from the Yankees earlier that year. At age 40, he ended up with the Braves and did not finish the '35 season.

Mother Teresa's real first name was Teresa.

Mother Teresa (1910–1997), born in Skopje (now in Macedonia), was named Agnes Gonxha Bojaxhiu. In 1929 she took the name of Teresa in memory of St. Thérèse of Lisieux. Mother Teresa was awarded the 1979 Nobel Peace Prize, which she accepted "in the name of the hungry, the naked, the homeless, of the crippled, of the blind, of the lepers, of all those who feel unwanted, unloved, uncared-for throughout society."

The place known as Purgatory, where souls are cleansed after death, is specifically mentioned in the Bible.

The Bible makes no mention of the place Catholics know as Purgatory. However, the Roman Catholic Church and many Christians believe there is a place where, after death, a soul must be cleansed. That place is Purgatory, which comes from the word *purge*.

Scotland Yard, the famous police organization, had its origins in the country of Scotland.

Scotland Yard, England's superb police organization did not have its origins in the country of Scotland. The name comes from the fact that its first headquarters were at "Scotland Yard," located in London. During the twelfth century Scotland was required to acknowledge its indebtedness to England by sending its kings to visit London where they stayed at their Scottish castle, which became known as Scotland Yard. Scotland Yard Police headquarters, established in 1829, moved from Scotland Yard to the Embankment, London, in 1890, and to Broadway in 1967. It has been called New Scotland Yard in these two latter locations.

The Klondike is in Alaska.

The Klondike is not in Alaska. The Klondike is located in the Yukon, a territory in Canada where in 1896 gold was discovered by George Carmack and his relatives. The Klondike region's proximity to Alaska has created the notion that it is located in Alaska. The stampede of prospectors heading for the Klondike region came through Alaska. Also, in 1899, there was a discovery of gold in Nome, Alaska, and another discovery in Fairbanks in 1902.

Penguins are found at the North Pole.

Penguins are not found at the North Pole. In fact, they are not found in the Northern Hemisphere at all. Penguins are found near the South Pole. A human outpost has the only animal life at the South Pole itself; the rest is closer to Antarctica's coastline. Offsetting the penguins, polar bears are found at the North Pole, not the South Pole.

The Canary Islands are so named because of their enormous bird population.

The word *canary* in Canary Islands had nothing to do with birds. The group of seven islands, which are located in the Atlantic Ocean and belong to Spain, takes its name from the Latin word *canis*, which means "dog." The islands, in ancient times, were populated with wild dogs.

The Greek ruins whose skeletal structure and pillars are seen standing in modern Athens were left that way from ancient times.

The skeletal structures and pillars so often seen by tourists who visit Greece were unearthed during various excavations in the last century and resurrected.

Big Ben is the name of the famous clock in the British House of Commons.

Big Ben in not the name of the famous clock in the British House of Commons, but the nickname of the *bell* in the clock tower. Big Ben weighs 13.8 tons and strikes on the hour. The bell is named after Sir Benjamin Hall, London's Commissioner of Works in the mid-nineteenth century. It was made by Whitechapel Bell Foundry, which also made the Liberty Bell.

Cotton is native to the American South.

Cotton is not native to the South, despite the existence of the Cotton Belt — a region in the South where much of the U.S. crop is grown. Cotton existed in prehistoric times in such countries as India, China, and Egypt, where it was used to make fabrics, carpets, and other textiles. In the first century A.D., cotton found its way to Europe, notably Italy, as Rome became the center of the world. Cotton became the South's principal crop, a crop the South depended on slaves to pick.

In Hollywood, California, the famous hillside Hollywood sign was so named when it was first erected on Mt. Lee in 1923.

The world famous Hollywood sign in Hollywood, California, was not so named when it was originally built. It once read HOLLYWOODLAND, not HOLLYWOOD. Hollywoodland on Mt. Lee, the highest place in Hollywood, was a housing complex, and the sign was an advertisement for it. No one really paid attention to the sign until 1932 when actress Peg Entwistle committed suicide by jumping off the *H*. The Hollywood housing complex didn't succeed, and in 1949 the word *land* was removed from the sign. The truncated sign, now reading HOLLYWOOD, has since become a Hollywood landmark.

The official language of Brazil is Spanish.

The official language of Brazil is Portuguese, because of strong Portuguese influence in the sixteenth century when that nation's explorers set foot in the country. Incidentally, when the Brazilian Republic was declared in 1889, it was called the United States of Brazil, and the government structure was based on that of the United States of America.

The country of Israel has the largest Jewish population in the world.

The United States, not Israel, has the largest Jewish population in the world. The U.S. has approximately 6 million people who identified themselves as Jewish in the 2003 census, whereas Israel has just around 5 million.

The Plains of Abraham are sacred lands located in the Middle East.

The Plains of Abraham is a large region overlooking Quebec City, Canada. In 1759 during the French and Indian War, the English under Gen. James Wolfe defeated the French under Gen. Louis Joseph de Montcalm at this site. The battle led to British supremacy in Canada. The region is lush with verdant meadows and is now a park (Battlefield Park) administered by the Canadian government.

The largest amount of U.S. gold is stored at Fort Knox, Kentucky.

The largest amount of U.S. gold reserves is to be found at Manhattan's Federal Reserve vault at Wall Street in New York City. Only 2% of the gold there belongs to the U.S. — the rest is in foreign accounts. When the World Trade Center fell, teams of treasury and FBI and U.S. soldiers quickly descended on the area, securing the buildings and closing off the area. The reserves amount to billions of dollars in gold bullion, silver, and platinum. Fort Knox holds second place in the storage of U.S. gold.

Times Square in New York City has always been called Times Square.

Times Square was originally called Longacre Square. On April 8, 1904, the name was changed to Times Square. To mark the completion of the New York Times Tower, on New Year's Eve in 1907, an illuminated ball was lowered from the tower for the first time. Ever since, Times Square has become perhaps best known for marking the passage of time on New Year's.

The Great Wall of China is the only manmade structure that can be seen from space.

No one knows exactly how this misconception started, but the Great Wall of China cannot be seen from the Moon or anywhere else a few thousands miles beyond Earth's atmosphere. All that can be seen of Earth from space are water, clouds, and some vegetation.

Practices
& Customs

Shaving will cause hair to grow back faster and thicker.

Shaving will not make hair grow back faster or thicker. It only appears that way after the first few days because the hair regrowth emerges as blunt, stubbly hairs that are very obvious to the eye. The hair may also be darker closer to the root.

Drinking coffee will make an intoxicated person sober.

Though it is widely believed coffee will bring one out of an intoxicated state, it will not. It will, however, take you out of a groggy sleepy state and put you into an awake drunken state. Only the liver can leach the alcohol from the human body. The National Safety Council, which has conducted numerous studies on this topic, does not advocate drinking coffee to sober up. They advise avoiding driving, and they believe that drinking coffee will do more harm than good. If a person is sober, coffee, because it contains caffeine, will keep the person alert. But one who has become drunk should sleep it off.

The foil wrapped around the necks and tops of wine and champagne bottles is there because it's decorative and makes the bottle tamper-proof to people.

The foil on wine and champagne bottles is there to cover the cork so as to make it tamper-proof to whatever pests might live in a wine cellar.

Freezing food kills bacteria and viruses, making it safe for consumption.

Freezing food won't kill bacteria or viruses, although it slows their growth and does kill parasites. What you put into the freezer is more or less what you'll have once the item defrosted. Flash freezing is often used to make sushi safe to eat because it kills any parasites in the raw fish.

In Alaska, Eskimos make igloos out of snow and ice.

Most igloos are not made of snow or ice but of sod or moss built with driftwood or whalebone, especially in Alaska. Summer houses are often tents covered with animal skins. In Canada, some winter igloos are made with just snow and ice. The word *igloo* is Inuit for house, and it doesn't specify the building material.

Performing abdominal exercises will give you a flat stomach.

Misled by television infomercials, many people believe that if they perform exercises for their abdominal muscles, they will get a flat stomach. In fact, the only way to get a flat stomach is to reduce the fat around the midsection. This is accomplished by eating a healthy diet and burning calories through cardiovascular exercise (jogging or swimming, for example). Although abdominal training will build muscle in your midsection, it is only part of what it takes to have a flat stomach.

If you swallow chewing gum, it will stay in your system for seven years.

Science proves that after gum passes through the alimentary canal it's the same as any other food we swallow. It passes through the digestive system within 24 hours.

When hypnotized, a person goes into a deep trance and will do anything the hypnotist says. They may never come out of the trance.

Hypnotized people do not fall into deep trances in which they'll do anything they are told to do. Hypnotism does not work on many people, but those who can be hypnotized do not fall into a deep zombie-like trance. A hypnotist cannot make a person do anything against his or her will. No one has ever been stuck in a hypnotic trance. At most, the hypnotized person may fall into a natural sleep and wake up refreshed.

In England, the public schools are where those children whose parents can't afford private schools are educated.

In England, the term *public school* refers to a school that draws its students from all over rather than just the local area. Public schools are anything but open to the public at large. *Elite boarding schools* would be a more accurate description..

The English and Canadian holiday Boxing Day is so named because it honors that nation's prizefighters.

Boxing Day has nothing to do with prizefighters or the sport of boxing. The name stems from the time when churches donated money from alms boxes to the poor on the day after Christmas. Aristocrats, likewise, began giving gift boxes to their servants on that date. Celebrated on December 26, Boxing Day is now a national holiday and the day postmen, doormen, and other service people are rewarded by the public for fine service throughout the year.

High tea is a formal affair.

High tea, originally an English custom, came about in the late 1800s as a blue collar family dinner, not an aristocrat's afternoon party. High tea was not a formal tea, but a break for refueling the body after toilsome labor. Food served along with high tea is traditionally basic: bread, pasties, and sweet baked goods.

In Indian restaurants, you can eat Bombay Duck, which, like Peking Duck, is a seasoned duck dish.

If you feel in the mood for Peking Duck and it just so happens that you cannot find it on the menu of your favorite restaurant, you are in for a surprise if you decide to order Bombay Duck. What the waiter will bring is not duck but fish – a dried salted fish used as a relish that accompanies curry. It might also be listed under the name *Bummalo*.

Bathing is a cherished ritual in Japan because Japanese people are preoccupied with cleanliness.

In Japanese culture, the ritual of bathing is considered a recreational luxury, a time not devoted to cleaning one's self, but instead a time to discuss business, a time for social meetings, for intimate family gatherings, to discuss politics, and so forth.

THE WHOLE TRUTH

Russians celebrate the October Revolution in October.

The October Revolution, the coup d'etat by the Bolsheviks under Lenin, occurred in *November* 1917. It is called the October Revolution because in 1917 Russia was using the Julian calendar, which was thirteen days behind the Gregorian calendar used in Europe, so the event took place in October in Russia.

St. Valentine was the inspiration for Valentine's Day, observed on February 14, a day devoted to matters of the heart.

Long before there was a St. Valentine, or a St. Valentine's Day, the date of February 14 was a day sacred to the pagans. It was a celebration of the Roman goddess Juno, protector of women and young girls, and a time of love and courtship. The Roman Catholic Church replaced this pagan tradition with a Christian one. The name St. Valentine's Day implies there was only one St. Valentine, but there was more than one St. Valentine, two of whom were martyred during the reign of emperor Claudius (A.D. 41–54). Saint Valentine was put on the calendar of saints in A.D. 496. Old legend varies, but the pagan tradition involved matchmaking and love letters.

In Victorian times, only upper-class women wore corsets.

Corsets have a reputation as a lady's undergarment, but in Victorian times women of all classes wore corsets. Originally high fashion, the working class also adopted the style.

Drawing rooms, once found in the homes of the well-to-do, were so named because it was the place for cultivating art skills.

Drawing rooms, were so named because they were the place to which families could withdraw—the term is shortened from "withdrawing room"—for recreation and conversation, most often after the evening meal.

When shopping for clothing while traveling or on the Internet, a ladies' size 10 is basically the same in all countries.

There is no worldwide standard system of clothing size. If you are a size 10 in the United States, you will basically be a size 12 in the United Kingdom; C38 in Norway, Sweden, and Finland; 40 in Belgium and France; 38 in Germany and the Netherlands; 44 in Italy; and 44/46 in Portugal and Spain. However, even in the United States, a size 10 will vary from manufacturer to manufacturer.

A married person is responsible for his or her spouse's debt.

As long as all finances are kept separate, one is not liable for a spouse's debt.

A pound of precious metal such as gold or silver weighs the same as a pound of potatoes, feathers, or coffee.

A pound of precious metal, such as gold or silver, weighs less than a pound of such measurable items as potatoes, feathers, or coffee — the latter consisting of sixteen ounces (known as an *avoirdupois* pound). Precious metals are measured by the troy scale, which has twelve ounces in a pound.

Deliberately setting U.S. paper currency on fire is a violation of United States currency laws.

Deliberately setting U.S. paper currency on fire is not a violation of United States currency laws. There is nothing legally wrong with burning U.S. paper currency, so eccentrics who light cigars with hundred dollar bills are not breaking the law.

The U.S. Treasury department no longer prints two-dollar bills.

Contrary to popular belief, the two-dollar bill is still printed by the Treasury Department and can be obtained from many banks if requested. The two-dollar bill has often confused both merchants and consumers, many of whom have never seen the two-dollar bill and do not believe it is authentic U.S. currency. Some people consider the bill to be bad luck. One fact is certain: When making a purchase with the two-dollar bill, the inconvenience of questions arising can be expected. There are those who keep two-dollar bills on the hunch that the Treasury Department will discontinue printing such notes, resulting in the bill becoming a collectible.

Sayings &
Names

The saying "sweat like a pig" aptly describes what happens to pigs when they are subjected to hot conditions.

Pigs do *not* sweat at all. They lack sweat glands. Pigs cool off by rolling around in mud. The mud ponds found on farms, are specifically designed for swine. Humans may sweat over their entire bodies, but the expression "sweat like a pig" as applied to humans is a misnomer.

The expression "drinking like a fish," aptly describes what fish are doing as they take in water through their gills while swimming.

The old expression "drinking like a fish" does not apply to the way fish take in water. When fish swim, they are breathing, not drinking. The water that passes through a fish's gills contains oxygen which is necessary for a fish to sustain life, just as it is for humans.

Prizefighters are also called pugilists.

To refer to a prizefighter as a pugilist is correct only if the prizefighter fights with his fists, *without gloves*. The last famous pugilist prizefight took place on July 8, 1889, when the great John L. Sullivan knocked out Jake Kilrain in the 75th round of the World Heavyweight Championship in what was a bare-knuckled fight between pugilists. Thereafter, as established by the marquis of Queensberry, a prominent figure in British sporting circles, all fighters wore gloves in competition.

The Bible says "Money is the root of all evil."

The Bible does not say "Money is the root of all evil." What is said in Timothy 6:10 is: "For the love of money is the root of all evil." Note: The key word is *love*.

Winston Churchill, upon replacing Neville Chamberlain as Prime Minister of Great Britain in 1940, uttered in his inaugural speech: "I have nothing to offer but blood, sweat, and tears."

Winston Churchill's famous early World War II quotation to the people of Great Britain was: "I have nothing to offer but blood, toil, tears, and sweat."

**Colonel William Prescott said to the
American soldiers at the Battle of Bunker Hill,
as they lay in wait for the British,
"Don't fire until you see the whites of their eyes."**

There's no record of Prescott (or Putnam) saying this at the Battle of Bunker Hill, but there are records of both Prince Charles of Russia (in 1745) and Frederick the Great (in 1757) giving their troops similar instructions.

Horace Greeley was the author of the statement "Go West young man, go West."

The statement "Go West young man, go West," was made not by Horace Greeley, but by John Soule in 1851 in the Terre Haute *Express* newspaper. Some years later, in 1865, Greeley picked up on the Soule quote in an article he was writing for the New York *Tribune* concerning advice on settling beyond the Allegheny mountains: "Go West, young man, and grow up with the country." Note: The phrase "Go West," as in where the sun sets, was an old pre-Victorian expression which meant: to perish, die, disappear, or depart to faraway places.

Bank robber Willie Sutton said "I rob banks because that's where the money is."

In a television interview several years before his death, Willie Sutton denied ever making this statement. He claimed that a reporter had invented it and that he never said it. However, he did write a book called *Where the Money Is*.

The explorer Sir Edmund Hillary offered the statement "Because it's there" as his reason for climbing Mount Everest.

This famous statement, so often used by modern-day daredevils to justify their seemingly mad quests, did not originate from the lips of Sir Edmund Hillary who scaled Mount Everest in 1953. The statement was first uttered in 1923 by another Everest climber, George Leigh Mallory, who on a second attempt to climb Everest in 1924 lost his life near the summit. Mallory's body was discovered in 1999.

Author Charles Dickens, in his 1843 *A Christmas Carol*, originated the famous phrase "dead as a doornail."

Charles Dickens was not the first to use the expression "dead as a doornail." The expression appears in *A Christmas Carol*, to describe Ebenezer Scrooge's former partner, Jacob Marley. The expression is found in Shakespeare's *Henry IV, Part Two*. It also appears in earlier lesser-known works. The phrase has been in wide use ever since.

Football coach Vince Lombardi said "Winning isn't everything, it's the only thing."

Football coach Vince Lombardi never said "Winning isn't everything, it's the only thing." What the great Lombardi said was "Winning isn't everything but wanting to win is." That statement "Winning isn't everything, it's the only thing," was said by a girl quoting John Wayne's character, a football coach, in the film *Trouble Along the Way* (1953).

He or she "marches to the beat of a different drummer" is the correct quote from Thoreau's *Walden*.

The expression he or she "marches to the beat of a different drummer" is nowhere to be found in Henry David Thoreau's *Walden* (1854). What you will find is: "If a man does not keep pace with his companions, perhaps it is because *he hears* a different drummer. Let him step to the music which he hears, however measured or far away."

"People in glass houses shouldn't throw stones" is a famous phrase attributed to George Herbert.

"People in glass houses shouldn't throw stones" is not the expression George Herbert wrote three and a half centuries ago. The actual line goes "Whose house is of glasse must not throw stones at another." The key word is *another*. Herbert's meaning behind the expression is not only different, but also more thorough when you think of it.

The term *Iron Curtain* was coined by Winston Churchill.

The term *Iron Curtain*, often used to describe the ideological barrier between democratic and communist countries, was not coined by Winston Churchill, who used the term in 1946 at an American college. *Iron Curtain* was actually coined as a Soviet Russian reference in 1924 by Ethel Snowden, wife of the British Chancellor of the Exchequer, in her book *Through Bolshevik Russia*. Visiting Russia with a delegation from Great Britain, and having at last arrived in Russia (1920), she writes: "We were behind the *Iron Curtain* at last."

The address *comrade* was a designation that applied to Soviet citizens in the old Soviet Union.

The word *comrade* applied only to members of the Communist Party.

The name of the bacteria known as *salmonella* is derived from salmon, which easily becomes contaminated if not properly refrigerated or cooked.

The name *salmonella* is derived from the name of American veterinarian Daniel Elmer Salmon, who first discovered it in 1885. There are more than 1,400 different types of the bacterium salmonella; one of the most common forms of salmonella infection is food poisoning.

Marie Antoinette said, "Let them eat cake."

Queen Marie Antoinette of France (1755–1793) never made the heartless remark "Let them eat cake" in reference to the starving people of Paris who could hardly provide themselves the basic staple of bread. The remark has also been attributed to Madame Sophie, the daughter of King Louis XV. There is evidence that the French philosopher Jean Jacques Rousseau was the root of the true source of the remark. His book *Confessions*, written in 1740, before Marie Antoinette was born, and published in 1765 when she was an eleven-year-old child living in Austria, contains a remark that bears close resemblance and is attributed to an unnamed princess who advises the populace to eat *brioche* (the French word for sweetbread). Sadly, Marie Antoinette had many enemies, who pinned the cruel remark on her, a remark that poor scholarship helped nurture.

SAYINGS & NAMES

***Pale Face* was a name coined by the America Indians to describe the white man. Indians also invented the practice of scalping their victims.**

American Indians did not coin the phrase *Pale Face* to describe the white man. The term came from the white American author James Fenimore Cooper, and who, in such novels as *Last of the Mohicans* (1826), put the term into the mouth of his Indian characters. As for the barbaric act of scalping, the American Indians learned the custom from early white Dutch settlers, people who committed such acts in their native Europe. The British earl of Wessex scalped his enemies in the eleventh century. Hollywood created the notion that Indians invented the custom.

The word *Kleenex* applies to any cleaning or facial tissue.

The word *Kleenex* is a trademark of the Kimberly Clark Corporation, and they would be first to report that all facial tissues are not Kleenex, since Kleenex applies to napkins and other products procduced by the company, not just facial tissues. A facial tissue is a facial tissue; a Kleenex is not necessarily a facial tissue. The same is true of *Xerox* for photocopying and *Frigidaire* for refrigerators.

Xmas is a secular way of saying Christmas.

Xmas is not a secular way of saying Christmas, nor is it a secular attempt to take "Christ" out of Christmas. The misconception arises out of the modern use of the letter *X* as a means of crossing out unwanted information. The *X* in Xmas, however, is actually the Greek letter chi. Chi is the first letter of Christ's name written in Greek and has always stood in that language as a symbol for Christ. The use of *Xmas* as a simple abbreviation for Christmas dates from the twelfth century and has been in continuous usage ever since.

**The term *Pennsylvania Dutch*
applies to people in Pennsylvania who
are of Dutch ancestry.**

Pennsylvania Dutch people are of German, not Dutch descent, their ancestors having come from Germany in the seventeenth century to escape religious persecution. The word *Dutch* is a mispronunciation of the word *Deutsch*, which means German. When the Dutch came to America they settled in what today is called New York, which they called New Amsterdam.

The term *scot-free* has to do with the people of Scotland and their quest to be free from England.

The term *scot-free*, as any native of Scotland knows, has nothing to do with the land of Scotland or the desire of its people to be free of the British Crown. The word *scot* is a very old English name for a specific tax that was used to pay the town or village sheriff. *Free* referred to the fact that certain nobles didn't have to pay the tax. Thus, to be scot-free is to be free of the scot or tax. The term is widely used in the United States to describe when serious criminals are released with no penalty imposed, such persons having gone scot-free.

Scotch-Irish when applied to a person means that the person is of half Scotch, half Irish descent.

A person of Scotch-Irish descent is not half Scottish, half Irish; the term applies to the Scottish settlers (Lowland Presbyterian Scots) who inhabited Northern Ireland in the 1600s after they were driven off their homelands by the English. The phrase equally applies to the descendants of these original Scottish settlers who suffered from high rents, excessive taxation, crop failures, and continued religious persecution. Many of these people left what is today known as "Ulster Ireland" to settle in America.

Scotch tape is any kind of cellophane or transparent tape.

Scotch is a trademark of the 3M Company, where the tape was invented, and the term *Scotch tape* specifically applies to cellophane tape produced by 3M. Other companies who also sell cellophane tape use their own name. Incidentally, Scotch tape (originally Scotch Brand Cellulose Tape) got its name from an old ethnic slur suggesting stinginess. When it was first developed, Scotch tape lacked adequate adhesive on the sticky side.

The international SOS code of distress stands for *Save Our Ship*.

The international SOS code signal of distress does not stand for *Save Our Ship*, or for that matter, *Save Our Souls*, or *Stop Other Signals*. SOS does not stand for anything. Adopted as a code of distress by international agreement in 1908, SOS is an easily transmitted signal made up of three dots, three dashes, and three dots. The code was sent for the first time from the RMS *Titanic* as a desperate measure, nevertheless proving futile. Note: SSS was used in World War II by torpedoed submarines.

The distress call *mayday* is the same as SOS and gets its name from May Day (May 1).

The distress call *mayday* is not the same as SOS, nor does it have anything to do with May 1—celebrated as May Day in some countries. Mayday is specifically a spoken distress signal which means *help me*, and it comes from the French *m'aidez*.

Science & Health

Shooting stars are stars.

Shooting stars are not stars, but meteors, ranging in size from grains of sand to golf balls, burning up in Earth's upper atmosphere. When they burn, they give off a bright light. Meteoric dust is often left by passing comets. We see meteor showers when the Earth crosses the orbit of comets, which happens at least a couple of times each year.

Meteors and *meteorites* are different words that describe the same thing.

Meteors are the visible streaks of light created by space debris burning up in the atmosphere. A piece of space debris itself is referred to as a *meteoroid* and is generally a chunk of rock and/or metal. *Meteorites* are remnants of the debris that reach the surface of a planet. This happens rarely, and meteorites are usually small and don't cause much harm.

All stars are white and starlight is white light.

Stars come in different colors depending upon their temperature (blue stars are very hot, and red stars are cooler). Most stars are red stars, but they are usually too dim to see. Our own sun is yellow. White stars exist as well. Most stars appear white to us is because of the limits of our eyesight. Our eyes have sensors called cones, which detect color. The cones do not sense light if it is too dim, so the default color we perceive is white. If a star is very bright, however, our cones will distinguish it. There are some colorful stars we can see with the naked eyes, including blue Altair and blue-white Vega in the summer and red Antares in the winter.

A light year is a measurement of time.

A light year is a measurement of distance, not time (despite the fact that it has the word *year* in it). A beam of light will travel about 9,500,000,000,000 kilometers in one year. This *distance* is defined as a light year, or the distance light travels in a year. Incidentally, a light nanosecond is just shy of a foot.

The seasons are caused by the change in the distance between the Earth and the Sun.

The seasons are mostly due to the axial tilt of the Earth, not the distance between the Earth and the Sun, which plays a very minor role. In the Northern Hemisphere, the axis is tilted toward the Sun at the summer solstice and away from the Sun at the winter solstice. In the Southern Hemisphere, this is reversed. Longer, hotter days in the summer are also attributed to that fact that the Sun is higher in the sky, which means that the Earth absorbs more heat in a day. The reverse happens in the winter.

Lightning doesn't strike the same place twice.

Lightning can strike the same place twice, or three times, or much more often. In fact, big buildings such as the Empire State Building and the Sears Tower get struck many times a year by lightning. There is a joke that lightning never strikes the same place twice because a place is never the same after being struck.

During a thunderstorm, lightning occurs before thunder.

During a storm, lightning and thunder occur at the same time. When lightning strikes, the air around it becomes so hot that an explosion takes place. The thunder is the sound of this explosion, but because the speed of light (29,388 kilometers/second) is far greater than the speed of sound (331.3 meters/second), we perceive the lightning as occurring first.

Mammals only came into being after the dinosaurs died out.

Tiny mammals weighing less than a pound coexisted with the dinosaurs for more than 150 million years. Mammals remained small until 65 million years ago, after dinosaurs became extinct.

Human beings evolved from apes.

Humans did not evolve from apes. At best, apes and humans are distant cousins. About 6–10 million years ago, apes and humans evolved from a common ancestor, now extinct, which scientists refer to as "the missing link." Paleoanthropologists have made many discoveries of hominid ancestors, but they have not yet agreed on the exact species from which apes and humans have evolved.

We use only 10% of our brains.

There is no scientific evidence that we use only 10% of our brains. A person uses almost all of his or her brain throughout the course of a day. Brain scans show that we indeed use far more than 10%. But it is a nice fantasy that we all have far greater potential locked up inside us.

Humans die with the same number of bones in their bodies as when they were born.

The average human body has 200–208 bones. Babies have far more, but some of the bones fuse together as a person grows, and others ossify later out of masses that look like cartilage.

Once a person reaches adulthood, he or she will have more or less the same skeleton for the rest of his or her life.

The bones in your body contain living cells. Like most other cells in the body, bone cells are in perpetual turnover, which means that the human skeleton fully replaces itself every seven years.

A human clone is an exact duplicate.

Just as identical twins are different from one another, so are clones. Sharing the same DNA does not produce the same person. People are more than a product of their genes, so a clone would vary just as identical twins (who are natural clones stemming from the same egg) do. The environment and a person's life experiences contribute to the formation of a unique individual.

THE WHOLE TRUTH

A common symptom of a person with Tourette's syndrome is constant cursing.

Although it has become known as the "cursing disease," most people with Tourette's syndrome do not voice obscenities; only about 10–15% of people with the disease reveal these symptoms. Tourette's syndrome is a neurological disorder that may cause involuntary motor and vocal tics, but those tics are not usually obscenities.

A person with schizophrenia has a split personality.

Schizophrenia, a severe mental illness, is not associated with a split or multiple personality. The misconception comes from the word *schism*, which means "split". The word *schizophrenia* describes the split between reality and mental illness. Schizophrenia is marked by visual and auditory hallucinations, and delusions and is currently treated with drugs and psychotherapy.

Only men have Adam's apples.

Men and women both have Adam's apples; however, they tend to be more defined on men. An Adam's apple is nothing more than enlarged thyroid cartilage running over the outer part of the larynx (voice box). The thyroid cartilage is usually the same size in boys and girls until puberty, when males' voices deepen and their larynx muscles enlarge, hence the appearance of a larger Adam's apple among men.

The skin infection known as ringworm is caused by a tiny worm.

Also known as *tinea*, ringworm is a fungal infection and is not related in any way to a worm. Ringworm or tinea appears on the skin as a red, scaly, ring-shaped patch. If the fungal infection is on the foot, it is called *tinea pedis* (also known as athlete's foot).

Athlete's foot gets its name because only athletes get it.

The fungal infection known as athlete's foot or *tinea pedis* is not particular to athletes. Athlete's foot was a catchphrase used by Absorbine Jr. Company (1928) to attract people who might frequent public baths, showers, swimming pools and locker rooms. Symptoms include itching and rashes, especially between the toes.

Copper bracelets cure arthritis.

Copper bracelets do not cure arthritis. The copper bracelet hoax continues to infiltrate generation after generation, in spite of countless warnings and reminders by medical authorities and consumer groups.

A drowning person will rise to the surface only three times before drowning.

A drowning person may not rise to the surface of the water at all, or may rise any number of times before drowning. How many times a person surfaces depends on the amount of air in the person's lungs and the rate that the stomach fills with water.

You can catch a cold by going outside in cold weather with inadequate clothing.

A cold is caused by personal contact with the living virus, not by simply getting cold. We catch more colds when it's cold outside, because we spend more time indoors in close proximity to one another. The best way to avoid catching a cold is to wash your hands frequently.

Hay fever is caused by hay.

Hay fever is caused by pollen, especially ragweed, which grows in the vicinity of hay fields. It is also not a fever.

Pet fur causes allergies.

Pet dander (dead skin flakes), saliva, or urine/droppings cause allergies, but not pet fur. If you have allergies, you don't necessarily need to give your pet away — you just need to give your pet a wash. Regularly shampooing your pet's coat will do wonders to reduce this allergen.

20/20 vision is the highest standard for perfect eyesight and also indicates healthy eyes.

20/20 vision is neither the maximum nor the standard denoting perfect eyesight. 20/20 eyesight also does not mean that one has healthy eyes; it simply means that both eyes see at twenty feet what the normal eye can see at twenty feet. It does not refer to perfect vision, even though doctors call it 100 percent vision. It also doesn't comment on peripheral, night, or color vision, or floaters, blind spots, or early onset of eye diseases.

The avocado is a vegetable.

The avocado contains a seed and is a fruit, not a vegetable.

Breadfruit
is a wheat product.

Breadfruit is not a wheat product, but a tropical fruit, so named
breadfruit because when baked the fruit looks and tastes like bread.

Like olives, bananas have oil in them, and this oil is called *banana oil*.

There is absolutely no oil in bananas. Banana oil is a synthetic compound (amyl acetate) that comes from petroleum. It is called banana oil because it has the odor of bananas. It is used as a flavoring agent in food and cosmetics.

Gelatin makes finger nails grow stronger, healthier, and more beautiful because it is a good source of protein.

Gelatin is a poor source of protein, and there is no scientific proof (no matter what the health food stores claim) that gelatin enhances nail beauty, strength, or length. Only a healthy, balanced diet will give one healthy nails.

After death, the nails and hair of the deceased continue to grow.

There is a reason why many people believe that a deceased's person's nail and hair grows after death. Nails and hair appear to grow because the skin recedes. This creates the illusion of nail and hair growth.

Ivory, like the ivory tusks of elephants, is naturally white.

Ivory is naturally discolored and must be bleached white (similar to teeth).

Mother-of-pearl is always white. Only the oyster produces mother-of-pearl.

Mother-of-pearl can be blue, gray, and even green. In addition to the oyster, the mollusk known as the abalone and the pearl mussel also produce the shiny, luminescent mother-of-pearl.

To distinguish between real and fake diamonds, we know that only real diamonds will cut glass.

Fake diamonds of several varieties will also cut glass. Only a gem expert can tell the difference between real and fake diamonds.

Dry ice melts.

Dry ice does not melt. It sublimates, skipping the liquid form. We would use the word *boiling* or *evaporating* to describe the transition if it went from liquid to gas.

Natural gas has its own natural smell.

Contrary to popular belief, natural gas is odorless. It is artificially scented for safety reasons.

**The word *ain't* is not in the dictionary.
The word's usage is considered incorrect by all
authorities on English language.**

The word *ain't* is in the dictionary. Ain't is a nonstandard phrase
meaning "am not," "is not," or "are not." The usage of the word *ain't*,
while it sounds incorrect, is defended by some authorities of the
English language as a correct colloquial contraction. Some examples
from *Random House Webster's College Dictionary* include "Ain't it the
truth!," "She ain't what she used to be," and "That just ain't so!"

The machines on airliners that record conversations in the cockpit (flight recorders) are called *black boxes* because they are black in color. Such machines are located in the cockpit of planes.

The famous *black boxes* on airplanes are not black at all, but *orange* for high visibility. There are two orange boxes on each plane. They are very sophisticated machines: one records flight data, the plane's air speed, altitude, and direction; the other box contains a machine designed to record cockpit conversations on a continuous looped tape that is thirty minutes long. Both are located in the tail section of the airliner (so they are more likely to survive a crash) and they are said to be virtually waterproof and able to withstand a 2,000-degree fire for a half hour. The machines have special batteries that are so powerful they will send out beeps from a crash site for over a month on land or sea. Once recovered, the flight recorders clarify what caused the accident. The term *black box* may refer to the fact that early recorders were painted black, or that charring after a crash often blackened the boxes.

Patent leather is genuine leather, most often from the hide of a horse or cow.

Patent leather is not real leather. It comes from a manmade process that most often uses plastic or vinyl. The procut is named "leather" because it so often has the look and feel of the real thing. First created by Seth Boyden in the 1810s, his invention is named after the United States patent office. Unlike patent leather, genuine leather is always made from the hides of animals.

SCIENCE & HEALTH

Hamburgers were originally made of ham, not beef.

The hamburger dates from as far back as the Middle Ages, when the Tatars (or Tartars), a band of nomadic warriors from Central Asia, developed a method for tenderizing raw beef by placing it under their saddles while they rode. This recipe eventually made its way to the German port of Hamburg, where the locals added their own seasonings, formed the beef into patties, and then fried or broiled it. In the nineteenth century, German immigrants brought their "Hamburg-style" beef to the United States. Served inside a hard roll, it caused a sensation at the 1904 St. Louis World's Fair and quickly became known across the nation as the hamburger.

Ulysses S. Grant is buried in Grant's Tomb.

Grant's Tomb contains Ulysses S. Grant and his wife, but the couple is not buried. They are entombed aboveground.

Camel hair brushes are made from camel hair.

Camel brushes, like Fuller brushes, are named for their inventors. Camel hair brushes are traditionally made from squirrel hair.

Cotton in bottles of aspirin is placed there by manufacturers to assure product freshness.

The cotton is placed in bottles of aspirin and capsules to prevent shaking of the bottles' contents, which would result in the chipping of tablets into fragments. Now that many aspirins are chip-resistant, this practice is stopping.

The Woodstock festival (1969) was held at Woodstock, New York.

Contrary to popular belief, the so-called Woodstock music festival was held on the vast farm of Max Yasgur, in the middle of the town of Bethel, quite a distance from Woodstock. The event was supposed to take place in Wallkill, but because of hastily created stringent rules, the planners were forced to pull out at the last minute. They turned to Bethel because getting a music festival permit was cheap and uncomplicated. The production company was named after Woodstock, New York, where the festival was never planned to occur.

White chocolate
is real chocolate.

White chocolate, the vanilla-flavored candy sold by chocolate makers, is not real chocolate. Real chocolate is made with cacao bean or seed, which gives it the brown color. White chocolate has no cacao beans and is actually white confectionary coating. To give white chocolate a chocolate flavor, candy makers add cocoa fat and vanilla ingredients found in real chocolate.

Eating chocolate causes acne.

Contrary to popular belief, eating chocolate—or any other fatty foods for that matter—does not cause acne. The only way chocolate might induce acne would be if it were rubbed on the skin until it clogged the pores.

Eating turkey makes you sleepy.

The turkey isn't responsible for diners' drowsiness after a Thanksgiving dinner. Turkey does contain the amino acid tryptophan, which can have sedating effects, but tryptophan is only sleep-inducing when consumed in large amounts on an empty stomach. Scientists consider the amount of tryptophan consumed during a typical Thanksgiving too minimal to have any noticeable effects. Post-meal lethargy can be attributed to eating too many carbohydrate-rich foods and drinking alcohol.

Eating late at night will make you fat.

Scientists have determined that there is no link between weight gain and eating late at night. The origin of this myth may have more to do with the types of food that people are likely to eat late at night in front of the television – fattening snacks such as potato chips, popcorn, and ice cream,

Reading in the dark will damage your eyesight.

While reading in the dark is likely to cause temporary eyestrain and fatigue, sometimes resulting in headaches, it will not permanently damage your eyes. Watching television in the dark is also not damaging to the eyes.

THE WHOLE TRUTH

C

H

I

T

Y